A Medal t

Story by Jan Weeks
Illustrations by Meredith Thomas

Contents

Chapter 1	The Trip Home	4
Chapter 2	Crash!	10
Chapter 3	What to Do?	16
Chapter 4	Searching for Help	22
Chapter 5	Help at Last!	28

Chapter 1
The Trip Home

"Are you asleep, Molly?" Dad asked.

"No," I answered, drowsily shaking my head. But I could feel myself drifting off to sleep. Apart from a quick stop for lunch, we'd done nothing but sit in the car since morning.

"How much further to go now, Dad?" I asked, probably for the hundredth time since we'd left Grandma's house in the city.

Dad smiled, "I guess we're about halfway. We should be coming to the turn-off soon."

The attendant at the service station had told Dad about a short cut that would reduce our trip home by an hour. It was just before Dad rang Mum to let her know we'd be another few hours.

Dad had to use the service station telephone because he'd left his mobile phone at Grandma's house. He was always forgetting things!

The short cut had been the best news I'd heard all day! Long car trips are so boring. If it hadn't been Grandma's birthday, I would've stayed at home. But she'd have been disappointed if I hadn't gone to her party.

Mum had stayed home. She was expecting a baby in a month's time and everyone said the trip would be too tiring for her.

"This must be the turn-off now," Dad said, as he swung the steering wheel to the left.

Not long after that, the road turned to dirt. "Why didn't that attendant tell me about this?" Dad grumbled.

It was getting darker and it had started raining. I closed my eyes, wishing I could sleep to make the trip seem shorter.

Chapter 2

Crash!

I awoke with a jolt. There was something wrong! Before I realised what was happening, there was an ear-splitting crash … then, everything went quiet.

I gathered my thoughts, and suddenly knew. Our car had slid sideways across the wet road and crashed into a tree.

"Dad!" I cried, but he didn't answer. I shook his shoulder. He moaned. "Dad, are you all right?" I asked softly.

"Are you?" he answered.

Apart from feeling shocked and shaken, I wasn't hurt at all. Dad's side of the car had taken most of the impact.

"I think I hit a pothole." Dad's voice sounded different — soft and strained at the same time. "My legs are trapped under the steering wheel, Molly. I can't move them."

"Oh Dad! What are we going to do?" I asked, feeling helpless. The rain was pelting down and the car headlights no longer worked — everything was dark.

"Wait," Dad answered. "And hope someone comes."

"What if no one comes?" I said, swallowing hard to keep back tears. We were on a dirt road, somewhere in the countryside, miles from the highway. Who would come down this short cut?

"Someone will," Dad whispered. "We just have to be patient."

"If only we hadn't left the mobile phone at Grandma's," I cried. "We could've rung someone. Like the police or the ambulance. Or Mum. She'd know what to do."

But Dad had gone to sleep.

I felt alone and frightened. Let someone come soon …

Chapter 3
What to Do?

Time passed ... and no one came. Dad groaned in his sleep. I knew he was badly hurt — when I'd reached across to hold his hand, it had felt sticky, so I guessed he was bleeding.

I didn't know what to do. Should I leave Dad and search for help? But it was dark outside, and I was scared of the dark. And what if I couldn't find anyone to help us? What if something happened to me? "Let a car come soon," I begged.

But no car came.

I remembered that Dad kept a torch in the glove compartment. I climbed into the front seat and, fumbling in front of me, found the catch. The door sprung open and the torch fell into my lap. At least now I could see!

But the light only confirmed that Dad needed help, and he needed it soon. What if he died while I sat beside him doing nothing? I knew I had to get help.

Dad opened his eyes and slowly turned his head towards me. "I'm sorry, Molly," he said slowly. "I didn't mean for this to happen."

"It wasn't your fault, Dad," I answered. "But I think I should go for help. You're hurt and you need an ambulance to take you to hospital."

"Wait until it gets light," Dad pleaded. "It's still raining and I don't want you wandering around in the dark."

I shook my head; daybreak was hours away. "I'll be as quick as I can," I said, and kissed his cheek. "I love you, Dad, and I won't let you down."

Dad was too weak to argue. I opened the car door and climbed out into the rain. I shivered as the rain sprinkled my face. At least it wasn't as heavy as it had been.

The dirt on the road was turning into mud, and I kept stepping in puddles. Still, I knew it was best to stick to the road: less chance of getting lost, and roads had to lead to somewhere …

Chapter 4
Searching for Help

"I am not afraid of the dark, I am not afraid of the dark," I chanted as I trudged along, scarcely seeing where I was going. Shadowy trees lined both sides of the road. I stumbled over a bridge and some railway lines, and, tripping over a branch that had fallen across the road, I almost fell head first into the mud.

In all, I fell over three times, bruising my knees and grazing my palms. I was sore and scared, but I kept on going. Dad was depending on me and I couldn't let him down.

Eventually, the rain stopped and patches of sunlight peeped through the clouds. Dawn was breaking and, at last, behind a fence I could see a house. My heart beat faster as I ran towards it. It was the best sight I'd ever seen.

But as I tried to open the front gate, two big dogs came bounding towards me, barking and showing their teeth.

"Can someone help me?" I shouted, too scared to go into the yard.

There was no reply. Oh no! What if no one was home?

Chapter 5

Help at Last!

I shouted again, and soon a woman appeared at the front door. She was looking out to see why her dogs were making such a fuss.

"We've had an accident," I called to her. "My dad's trapped in the car. He needs help."

After that, the woman quietened the dogs, took me into the house, and immediately rang for an ambulance to go and get Dad.

Then she made me change into some of her daughter's clothes while she fixed me a warm drink. I couldn't stop shaking.

"It's shock," said the woman, putting a blanket around my shoulders, "as well as the cold."

We got into her car and drove back down the road to find Dad.

I couldn't believe how far I'd walked. Neither could the woman.

When we arrived, the ambulance officers were already helping Dad.

He was lying on the ambulance stretcher. It was so good to see him!

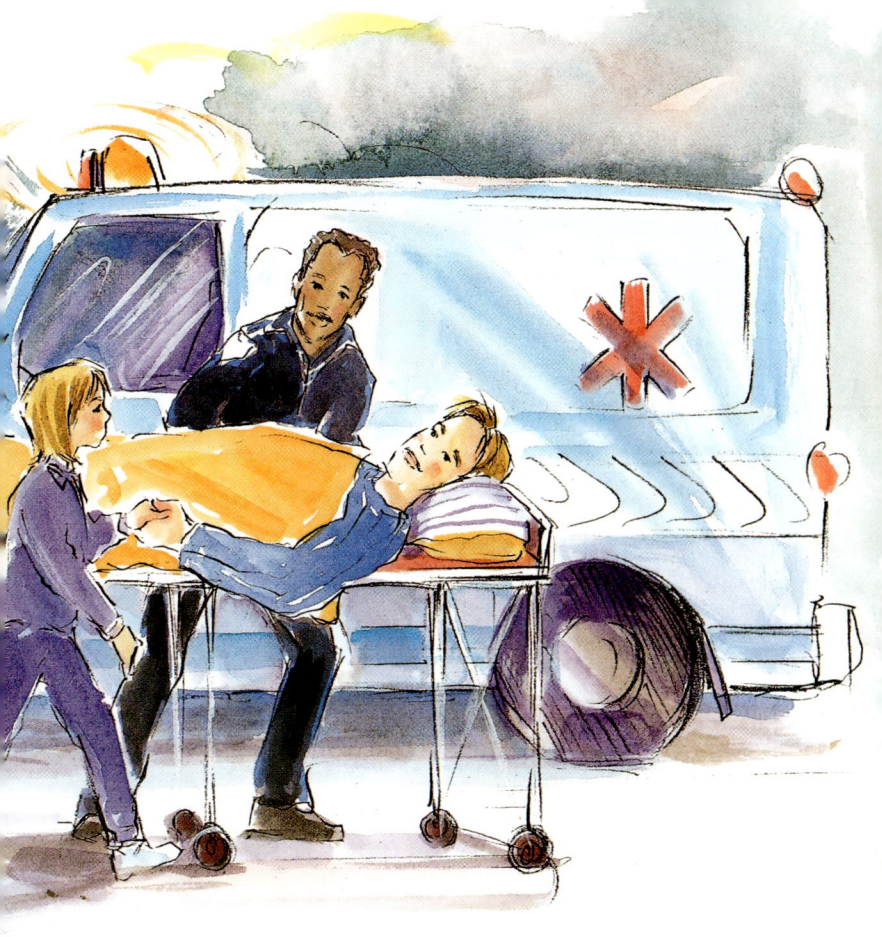

One of the officers said that Dad was going to be okay. He had a fractured leg and a lot of cuts and bruises. One of the cuts was deep and Dad had lost a lot of blood.

"Thank goodness you went for help, Molly," said Dad, squeezing my hand.

"You're a very brave girl to do what you did for your father," said a police officer. "I think you deserve a medal!"

But I didn't care about being brave, or about medals. I was just glad it was all over, and that Dad was going to be all right.